CHRISTMAS

FOR

ANGELO

BY

ROBERT M. PALAZZO

ILLUSTRATION

BY

ERNEST DUONOLA

Archway Publishing books may be ordered through booksellers or by contacting:

Archway Publishing
1663 Liberty Drive
Bloomington, IN 47403
www.archwaypublishing.com
1-(888)-242-5904

ISBN: 978-1-4808-0679-5 (sc)
ISBN: 978-1-4808-0678-8 (e)

Printed in the United States of America

Archway Publishing rev. date: 4/9/2014

I want to thank my wonderful wife Janine

My two sons Michael and Robert

And my Grandson Angelo

For their inspiration

And belief in this book.

Also

My mother Frances

My father Enea

My brother Salvatore and sister Doreen

And my family

For helping to mold me into the person that I am.

Also

My mother in law Marie

And brother-in-law Ernest

Wow, lots of strange goings on around here, lots of excitement. I vaguely remember something like this about a year ago, but I was too young then to realize what was going on. I'm much older now and I sense something different is going on than the normal. Hi, my name is Angelo; I am 16 months old. There is something in the air. I can feel it. The adults are really starting to act strange. Everyone seems so much happier, and full of joy. Too much for my young mind to take in: lots of nice Christmas music everywhere, people laughing, bundles and boxes being moved here and there. What is this Christmas thing I keep hearing about?

Things my grandpa shows me like the stars in the sky look like they are everywhere now. There is a tree in my house with those twinkling stars from the sky on the tree. What is a tree doing in my house? Grandpa always shows me the trees outside in the yard and other places. How did grandpa get those stars that are so far away in the sky, down here and spread all over the place? I am really getting confused. Somebody has some explaining to do! Where are my grandpa and grandma, mommy and daddy with answers when I really need them?

Oh okay, I am starting to see things a little clearer now. On Sunday we went down the city to Macy's to see this Santa Claus guy. I mean we just got finished with Thanksgiving and here we go again. Well anyway what a set-up this Santa Claus guy has. I think somehow he is connected to this Christmas holiday. It may take me a while but I think I will get it eventually. Well anyway, when we were at Macy's there was so much craziness. Hustle and bustle, arms full of boxes and bags; anyway back to Santa Claus.

Grandma has been showing me Christmas movies; so I am starting to understand a little better. We went to see Santa; he was a little scary at first. I wouldn't sit on his lap, but I did sit next to him. We had to take some pictures. All of a sudden grandma asked me did I see Santa; and I come out with ho, ho ho, where did this come from? Everybody starts laughing so I go for it again with my deep voice and real slow ho, ho, ho. I guess I got it from the movies we have been watching, I don't know, oh boy I'm getting confused again.

Santa looked a little familiar now, thanks to my grandma for watching those movies with me. Anyway back to Macy's, we had to go through a couple of different rooms to get to see Santa. Many Christmas trees, toy trains, elves, toy soldiers taller than my dad and grandpa. Lots of nice decorations to see; Santa was pretty scary at first, really big, lots of white hair and a long white fluffy beard. I wouldn't go near him without my dad and mom, but after a couple of minutes it seemed like he was going to be okay. I knew I was safe with my mommy and daddy. Well we sat and chatted, I guess just some gibberish on my part, well he asked me what I wanted…. mmm I was thinking, maybe you can tell me what this Christmas is all about. We took some pictures and than on our way. Somehow I know this is all going to fit together.

I was sitting in my high chair on Monday waiting for dinner, and I heard this voice on television saying they are going to lightning an eighty foot Christmas tree filled at rocket filled center. Lightening, rockets, what's going on here? Oh, light an eighty-foot Christmas tree at Rockefeller center: that sounds better and make some sense, I guess. I watched it on television, wow, was that tree BIG! Lots of lights looked like more stars to me, really pretty and a lot of different colors. Mommy told me we were going down to see the tree. Going down to where ma? You need to fill me in. There is a lot to think about here. After all I am just a baby. Now, I really need to know how many Santa's there are. Every time we are out I see a different Santa somewhere else.

Is this how he gets to everyone's house in one night? And what's with all the ringing bells? Every time I see a Santa or a Christmas tree I start with the ho, ho, ho. It just comes out, like I can't stop myself. Every body keeps laughing; I mean that is going to get old quick, but I will continue to ho ho ho until it stops being cute. So anyway, this is the big night we are going down to see the biggest Christmas tree of all at Rockefeller center. The big night of the departure to see the tree was exciting; dad, mom, grandma, grandpa, my two uncles and great grandma were all set to go. I'm thinking it wasn't their first time to see the tree but it was mine, and I was really happy. We got into a couple of cars and headed out. Dad had Christmas songs playing on the car radio, really festive and nice. It seems like it took an awful long time to get there, but when they took me out of the car it was like WOW! People everywhere, music, lights, stars so many pretty and wonderful things. We walked for a while, I wasn't walking, too much of a crowd for me, I was in grandpa's arms. Now this is the way to travel.

Ho
Ho Ho Ho
Ho
Ho
Ho
Ho
Ho
Ho
Ho

We were getting close I can tell more and more people, and everyone was walking faster. Grandpa told me to close my eyes for a big surprise…and when I opened them, there it was an 80-foot Christmas tree. What is 80 foot? What does that really, really mean? I had to look way up in the sky to see the top of the tree. Daddy took me and put me on his shoulders so I could see the tree better, not like I couldn't see it from where I was. I could probably have seen it from my house it was so big, WOW! It really was nice and all the different colors and lights, it is really something I am going to remember for a long, long time. There were so many people taking pictures, looking around and being happy. It was a really good night, with mom, dad, grandma, grandpa, uncle and uncle and great grandma.

We did a lot of walking, well I didn't I was being carried, good for me. We went to see the windows in Saks all decorated for Christmas. Lights, lights and lights everywhere beautiful figurines moving and trains going round and round. So many different and Christmassy things to see. I heard a lot of oohs and aahs, so I guess people were liking it. Okay, almost time for the ride home, probably naptime for me…yea I have just about had it; I am exhausted. I'm glad it was dad's turn to drive and not mine, ha ha.

Okay we need to move the season along here, no time for all the small details. I keep hearing about presents and real nice things Santa is supposed to be bringing me. How does all this work, and when does it happen? Christmas, Christmas Eve when does it come? I have some sort of calendar with all the days of the month with chocolate candy in them that daddy keeps eating on me. He told me I'm too young for the chocolate, mmm I wonder. I think dad is tricking me here. I thought that was for me, anyway, not many windows left to open so we must be getting close to this Christmas day, we are all waiting for, well I am anyway. I want to get to the end of all this, everyone is really getting anxious and it's starting to affect me.

THE MOONLIGHT FELL ON THE SNOW, MAKING IT LOOK LIKE A SUGARY CONFECTION.

Okay next thing I hear is where we are going for Christmas Eve and Christmas day. What do you mean? Where do we have to go? Grandma and Grandpa do Christmas Eve, than mom's family, Christmas day. It sounds like a lot of coming and going again. Grandma and grandpa make all the fish. What fish? Is grandpa going to empty his fish tank? Okay, I found out we won't be eating the fish in the tank; we will be eating seven fishes. This is a tradition at grandma's and grandpas on Christmas Eve. I really didn't get any of the fish, but only had macaroni and the gravy was fish sauce and it was really good. I can't wait till I can get more. Mmmm, grandma is some good cook.

On Christmas day when I woke up, mommy and daddy were all excited; they said Santa had visited our house last night, and left a lot of presents for me. The choo-choo was running around the Christmas tree, dad had Christmas music playing. I was really getting excited. There were so many presents in the living room for me. Toys, toys, toys were everywhere I didn't know where to go first. Dad was helping me and mom was taking pictures. I had toy cars, trains, puzzles, books too many things to name. Was all this mine? Dad said because I was a good boy Santa brought me lots of gifts and they were all mine. He said there were lots of gifts at grandma and grandpas and my other grandma's and all our other relatives and friends. Wow I'm thinking this Christmas thing is all pretty good.

TRUCK

All the mystery is done. It all tied together. All that we did, going to the city, seeing all the decorations, all the visiting and Santa, and all that we did before and now that Christmas is here. Seeing everyone in my family, and all their friends this time of the year is really a happy time. A time of fun and a time of joy. A time I want to have a lot more of. To bad Christmas isn't everyday: not just for the presents, but all the fun and joy and visits. Too bad Christmas comes but once a year. Ho Ho Ho.

Angelo

I have a new twinkle in my eye
He is more than I need to get by
Every face that he makes
Is like a new picture to take.
I wonder what he thinks
In his little head
As I sit and watch him
As he lay in his bed,
He can light up a room
With a little smile
He makes my heart flutter
And stand still for a while.
I never realized how wonderful
A grandson could be,
He is all so precious
And so beautiful to me,
I will treasure the moments
As he learns and grows
I will always be there for you
My little Angelo.

Angelo Again

As I sit and watch you lying there
I have to kiss your face
I have to touch your hair

You my Angelo, a little charm
I can't hold you tight enough in my arms

There is so much I love in life
My friends, my family,
My children, my wonderful wife

But now I've found a different and special love
This a love from heaven above
This love for you, my little boy
The love you are, my special joy

I can't explain the love I feel
I have to pinch you Angelo
To make sure you are real.

Our lives keep changing in so many ways
We turn the pages; the different days
But if this is all I am going to get

Thank you God, for this little boy
Thank you God for all my joy
I am so proud it has to show
Thank you God for my Angelo

Robert (Bobby) Michael Palazzo